Involvement in Cryptocurrencies is a risky proposition

Investing in Cryptocurrencies: A Step-by-Step Guide for Beginners Learn about tried-and-true investment strategies that can help you increase your profits significantly. As an added bonus, investing in non-financial institutions is recommended.

Roberta A. McCormick

Contents

Chapter One

Introduction

What makes cryptocurrency the most significant invention of this millennium is as follows. Digital currencies are the next step in the expansion of the global economy. The exchange of more value between countries and federations is analogous to the expansion of the economies they support when a seedling is transplanted into a larger container.

Countries have historically decoupled their currencies from the gold standard in order to improve their ability to circulate value. Countries and federations are severely restricted in their ability to act now that the gold standard has been removed from currency production. These countries' ability to support their own economies, as well as the amount of currency they can print in order to circulate value, are limited.

Introduction to the fundamentals of cryptocurrency trading, presented in an easy-to-understand format for those who are just getting started. Investing in the new currency is explained in detail in this book, which is an all-in-one resource for beginners. This guide will assist you in learning everything you need to know about trading, investing, and mining cryptocurrencies such as Bitcoin, Ethereum, Ripple, and Litecoin, as well as other digital currencies.

In spite of the fact that the cryptocurrency market is fraught with danger, it also provides the opportunity to make significant money. Make easy and legitimate money by investing wisely and employing strategies that are appropriate for your level of risk toleration. In this book, I go over the fundamentals of cryptocurrency investing, as well as the risks that come along with doing business in this space.

Investing in and trading in cryptocurrencies, as well as the underlying blockchain technology, can be intimidating for those who are new to the trading industry. Aiming to make trading information as straightforward and to the point as possible, this book This book will show you where to begin, how to begin, and how to establish a plan that works for you if you are new to cryptocurrency investing.

Although it has been popular for a few years, keep in mind that the cryptocurrency market is still in its early stages and thus suited for new investors. The only stumbling block to investing in cryptocurrencies is a lack of relevant and practical information on how to get started and enter this market. This book recognizes this problem and addresses it by giving you all the knowledge to get started. As you read this book, you will learn more. CHAPTER 1:

What Are Cryptocurrencies: Their Birth

Chapter Two

What Are Cryptocurrencies: Their irth

What distinguishes cryptocurrencies, though, is the technology that powers them. "Who cares about the technology underlying my money?" you may ask. I'm solely concerned about how much of it is in my wallet!" The difficulty is that the world's present money systems are riddled with flaws. Following are some examples:

Credit cards and wire transfers are antiquated payment methods.

In most cases, a slew of intermediaries, such as banks and brokers, take a piece of the action, making transactions expensive and time-consuming.

The global financial disparity is increasing.

Approximately 3 billion individuals are unbanked or underbanked and have no access to financial services. That equates to around half of the world's population!

Cryptocurrencies hope to solve some of these issues, if not all of them.

Understanding the Basics

You know that your regular, government-issued cash is kept in banks. And that you must have an ATM or a bank connection to receive more of it or transfer it to others. Well, with cryptocurrency, you might be able to do away with banks and other centralized intermediaries entirely. That is because cryptocurrencies rely on a decentralized technology known as Blockchain (meaning no single entity is in charge of it.) Instead, each computer in the network verifies the transactions.

Cryptocurrency History

Bitcoin was the first cryptocurrency ever created! You've undoubtedly heard of Bitcoin more than anything else in the crypto business. Bitcoin was the first blockchain product made by an unnamed individual named Satoshi Nakamoto. Satoshi Nakamoto proposed Bitcoin in 2008, describing it as a "purely peer-to-peer version" of electronic money. Although Bitcoin was the first official cryptocurrency, numerous attempts to create digital currencies years before Bitcoin was formally released.

Mining is the method through which Bitcoin and other cryptocurrencies are produced. Mining Bitcoins, unlike mining ore, requires powerful computers to solve complex issues.

Until 2011, Bitcoin was the only cryptocurrency. Then, as Bitcoin enthusiasts began to notice its weaknesses, they decided to build alternative coins, commonly known as altcoins, to improve Bitcoin's design in areas such as speed, security, privacy, and others. Litecoin was one of the earlier altcoins, striving to be the silver to Bitcoin's gold. However, there are over 1,600 cryptocurrencies accessible at the time of writing, with the number projected to grow in the future.

Some Advantages of Cryptocurrency

Still not convinced that cryptocurrencies (or any additional form of decentralized money) are preferable to conventional government-issued currency? Here are a few solutions that cryptocurrencies, because of their decentralized nature, may be able to provide:

Reducing Corruption

When you have a lot of power, you also have a lot of responsibility. When you give a lot of energy to just one person or entity, the odds of that person or thing misusing that authority grow. According to Lord Acton, a 19th-century British statesman, "Power corrupts, and absolute power corrupts absolutely." Cryptocurrencies seek to address the issue of absolute power by sharing authority among many persons or, better yet, among all network participants. That is, after all, the basic concept of blockchain technology.

Eliminating Extreme Money-Printing

Governments have central banks, and when faced with a significant economic situation, central banks can print money. That is also known as quantitative easing. By printing additional money, a government may pay off debt or depreciate its currency. This method, however, is like putting a bandage on a broken leg. It rarely solves the problem, but the harmful side effects can sometimes outweigh the initial issue.

When a country, such as Iran or Venezuela, issues too much money, the value of its currency plummets, causing inflation to spike and citizens to be unable to afford essential goods and services. Their money is worth about as much as a roll of toilet paper. In addition, most cryptocurrencies have a fixed number of coins accessible. When all those currencies are in circulation, there is no straightforward method for a central entity or the firm behind the Blockchain to generate more coins or add to its supply.

Giving People Charge of Their Own Money

You essentially hand over complete authority to central banks and the government with traditional cash. If you count your government, that's fantastic, but keep in mind that your government can quickly freeze your bank account and refuse you access to your funds at any time. For instance, in the United States, if you die without a valid will and own a company, the government inherits all of your assets. Some governments may even discontinue issuing

banknotes as India did in 2016. As a result, you and only you have access to your funds when using cryptocurrency. (Unless someone snatches them from you.)

Cutting out the Middleman

When you transfer traditional money, an intermediary, your bank, or a digital payment firm, gets a percentage. With cryptocurrencies, all network members in the Blockchain serve as the middleman; their compensation is structured differently from that of fiat money intermediaries, and so is minor in contrast.

Serving the Unbanked

Many of the world's citizens have no or limited access to payment systems such as banks. Cryptocurrencies hope to alleviate this problem by extending digital commerce worldwide, allowing anyone with a mobile phone to make payments. And, yes, mobile phones are more widely available than banks. More people own smartphones than toilets, but blockchain technology may not solve the latter issue at this time. CHAPTER 2:

Bitcoin and Its Uses

Bitcoin as Investment

The majority of people regard Bitcoin as a form of future investment. With its supply capped at twenty-one million coins and its relatively low price, there are many ways you can turn a profit just by investing in Bitcoin. While it is admirable if you want to play the Bitcoin market for quick profits, consider that losses can appear as quickly as profits.

You can also apply Bitcoin as an investment by including it in your future planning, not just as a way to make a quick gain. Bitcoin is still relatively new; it is fairly undeveloped, so there is plenty to discover. This makes Bitcoin a good investment portal, albeit a risky one.

Instructions on how to use bitcoins

People should be educated about Blockchain technology, and they should be shown how it has enormous potential for assisting them in maintaining control over their own money, according to my assessment. People's interactions with technology, as well as their perceptions of the rest of the world, are being altered as a result.

The presence of fraud may be found everywhere, as can poor management, constraints on financial resources, limitations on what constitutes free expression, and a slew of other issues that should not be tolerated in today's society. Cryptocurrency was originally envisaged by Satoshi Nakamoto to be an effective tool for spreading revolutionary forms of technology that would demonstrate to people how they might decentralize their whole lifestyle in order to live free of fraud and corruption.

So far, the majority of Bitcoin teaching has concentrated on the technical and financial elements of the cryptocurrency. With much more space for advancement, Bitcoin has the ability to make a significant difference in the lives of people. More than just technology and money are involved. Clearly, there is tremendous potential here! It is only when you have a thorough understanding of how Bitcoin and blockchains work that you will be able to appreciate the value they may bring to your daily life.

A plethora of options is available. Try to imagine how elections might be run without the presence of any genuine human observers for a few minutes. Think of the capacity to sign and save papers, to update and negotiate contracts, and to carry out peer-to-peer transactions. These are all possibilities. Using blockchain technology, it is possible to deliver all of these services in a safe and secure manner.

Consumption on a regular basis

People are mainly drawn to Bitcoin because it offers an online payment mechanism that is convenient and secure. A cheap cost, little danger of chargebacks or fraud, and the ability to complete transactions instantly are all reasons why businesses are starting to embrace Bitcoin as a payment method. As a result, Bitcoin is becoming more popular as a viable method of payment, both online and at a broad range of physical establishments throughout the globe. In today's world, the Bitcoin system is mostly used to transmit money anywhere in the globe, regardless of currency. However, the increasing adoption of the technology in the commercial world only serves to increase its long-term sustainability.

One intriguing alternative for spending Bitcoin reveals itself in the form of firms that bring meals to your doorstep. Starbucks and Domino's Pizza, two well-known coffee chains, now accept Bitcoin payments (PizzaForCoins.com.) Large-scale internet retailers such as Microsoft and Expedia are among the most successful. Payments for their services are accepted using Bitcoin by companies such as Dish Network, CheapAir, and Roadway Moving. In addition to restaurants, bars, museums, and other establishments, more than a thousand stores globally will accept Bitcoin payments as of this writing. If you do a fast search on the internet, you will discover that there are several methods to spend your Bitcoin.

Bitcoin and Exorbitant Expenses in the Luxury Sector

Rather from being a niche phenomenon, Bitcoin has drawn interest from individuals from a broad spectrum of backgrounds. A new financial invention is now open for participation by everyone, from millennials to inhabitants of poor economic zones. With Bitcoin, you can make reservations for hotels and flights. There are certain locations where you may even use it to pay bills or even to pay off traffic penalties. This procedure may be made easier by taking use of a variety of accessible services.

Customers who pay with Bitcoin are happy to spend a little bit more on their hotels and flights, according to the firms that take Bitcoin. If they spend more money, it might be because they feel more comfortable doing so, or it could be because the exchange rate was particularly bad at the time. It's unclear why, but it demonstrates that adopting Bitcoin is advantageous to both buyers and sellers.... This stays true regardless of the product or service that is being provided.

Bitcoin Is Accepted by Nonprofits.

Helping others, especially those in need, is a vital component of our human existence. A number of charitable organizations, including Greenpeace and the Red Cross, accept gifts made in Bitcoins. In addition, some organizations are willing to help donors in the process of deducting their Bitcoin payments from their taxes.

Since the invention of Bitcoin, you no longer have to depend on a third party to distribute your charitable contributions to those in need. Several individuals may, for example, donate Bitcoin directly to the Nepal Relief Fund after the 2015 earthquake in Nepal rather than funneling their gifts via charity organizations in their own countries. Since the Bitcoin contributions arrived swiftly on the scene of the tragedy, disaster personnel were able to address crucial needs right away rather than having to wait for money to arrive via more conventional channels.

Gambling on the internet is prohibited.

Given that sports betting and online gambling are still illegal in certain jurisdictions, you should be aware of any relevant restrictions and guidelines before engaging in any betting or online gambling activities. For those who live in jurisdictions where online gambling is legalized, Bitcoin is a speedier and more convenient method of payment than bank cards and/or electronic funds transfers (ACH).

To authenticate your identity using Bitcoin, you will not be required to give any personal information or any supporting proof. You will make a deposit and then you will be ready to begin playing! Bitcoin transfers are the preferred payment option for online casinos due to the fact that they are non-refundable and very quick. My conscience still encourages me to gamble responsibly, despite the fact that I accept the fact that you are an adult. That's all there is to it, really.

Investing in Precious Metals

Bitcoin may be used to purchase precious metals such as gold, silver, and other forms of silver. Trading Bitcoin against precious metals is possible via many sites. Current market leader Vaultoro is the most widely used online trading platform, and this platform is mostly concerned with Bitcoin and gold trading. Another three reliable exchanges where Bitcoin may be used to trade for precious metals are Uphold, Midas Rezero, and BitGold are all well-regarded. Before you invest any of your Bitcoin, be sure to study the firms you plan to employ and their track record in the marketplace.

Bitcoin may be given as a present.

There are several sites where Bitcoin can be swapped for gift cards, such as eGifter and Gyft, which make Bitcoin an excellent present for friends and family members. A large number of retailers accept Bitcoin payments, despite the fact that most do not take Bitcoin payments in their direct whole. Bitcoin, on the other hand, may be given as a present or used as a payment mechanism for other cards, due to gift cards.

Payments for Bills

It will depend on your location whether you will be able to pay your expenses using Bitcoin. People will be able to pay any of their bills using Bitcoin for a modest fee on a number of sites that are now being created.

Payments for your mortgage, phone, and utility bills will soon be feasible via the use of Bitcoin. For quite some time now, it has been possible to top up your mobile phone account with

Bitcoin, however this service is not currently accessible in all parts of the globe.

The Bitcoin Community is Growing!

Given that you have a genuine enthusiasm for bitcoin, you may be discouraged by its present lack of utility. What is holding you back from getting out and teaching customers and merchants about the many advantages they can gain from using and/or accepting Bitcoins? In order to fully develop the Bitcoin ecosystem, it will require a significant amount of time and work, and since there is no centralized authority in charge, it will be up to members of the Bitcoin community to spread the word and push for the acceptance of Bitcoin.

All of the Bitcoin applications discussed in this article represent just a tiny percentage of the many possible applications for Bitcoin.. In the Bitcoin ecosystem, coming up with unique applications for the virtual currency Bitcoin is quite valuable. Whenever you have the opportunity, it is also crucial to communicate with the community how you are using Bitcoin. THREE-THIRD CHAPTER

Blockchain

Chapter Three

Transparency on the Blockchain

Consider the case of a ledger that is duplicated hundreds of times over a network of computers. Now imagine that this network is designed to be updated on a regular basis, and you have the fundamental knowledge of blockchain technology at your fingertips.

Blockchain-stored information will persist as a publicly accessible and periodically reconciled database for the duration of the blockchain's existence. In this case, the network is being used in a way that provides obvious benefits. Rather of being held in a single place, the blockchain ledger is accessible to anybody who wishes to see or verify the information it contains. The data is not in a centralized format that may be stolen or compromised by an intruder or hacker. Because it is hosted by a large number of computers all over the globe at the same time, anybody may access the data on the Blockchain over the Internet.

When it comes to understanding this notion, if you are acquainted with Google Docs, it will be simple for you to grasp. To share papers with others for collaborative work, the traditional technique is to email the document to another person and request that they make some adjustments. The disadvantage of this technique is that you must wait until that individual delivers you a new copy of the document before you can view the modifications.

Our databases are now using this approach, and it is the most recent version available. The same document cannot be modified by two different users at the same time, for security reasons. Most financial institutions today manage, transmit, and preserve their customers' money balances in the manner described above. During a transfer, they temporarily lock the access to the record, wait for the other side to update the record, and then re-access the record to check for changes. Google Docs allows both users to work on the same document in real time if they are using the same Google account. Similar to a public ledger, however this is a shared record rather than a private ledger. When numerous persons are involved in the sharing, the dispersed component will be activated.

Aspects of Blockchain's resilience are similar to those of the Internet. A single point of failure is eliminated from the Blockchain, and a central authority is unable to govern it since blocks of data are kept similar throughout the network.

Bitcoin was created in 2008, and since then, blockchain technology has been operating without any significant interruption. Mismanagement and cyber-attacks are the primary causes of Bitcoin-related issues. To put it another way, these issues are the result of poor faith or human mistake, rather than the framework itself.

To put it simply, Blockchain is a technology that is designed to hold users accountable at the highest levels of governance. Thus, mistakes (both human and machine) as well as missing transactions will be a thing of the past in the near future. Last but not least, securing the veracity of a transaction through public record-keeping, not only on the primary register but on a linked distributed system of registers, which are all linked via a validation system that is immune to outside interference, is the most critical area in which Blockchain can be used to help.

The blockchain network exists in a consensus world of collective knowledge, in which automated checks and balances are performed every 10 minutes by a distributed ledger system. With the network's ability to reconcile each transaction that happens at 10-minute intervals, it may be considered a self-checking ecosystem of virtual value. A block is a collection of transactions that are all related to one another in some way, shape, or form. It is possible that this will result in the following two key characteristics:

As a result, updating any data on the Blockchain would take a massive amount of computational power to override the whole network, making it incorruptible.

It is possible to obtain data transparency since it is incorporated inside the network as a whole and therefore available to the general public in its entirety

Despite the fact that this is theoretically feasible, it is unlikely to occur in practice. In the same way, seizing control of the system in order to capture Bitcoins will have the same consequence of decreasing the value of the cryptocurrency.

In blockchain technology, nodes are known as the fundamental unit.

Nodes are the building blocks of the blockchain network. One kind of node is a computer that has been connected to the blockchain network via a client and is responsible for verifying and relaying transactions within the ecosystem. After joining the whole network, the Blockchain is instantly downloaded to each node's hard drive.

They combine to form a powerful second-level network, which represents a whole new model of how the Internet may function. In the Blockchain network, each node acts as the administrator and does so willingly. There is no centralized management of the network as a result. However, as a thank you for participating in the system, each node is given the opportunity to earn Bitcoins.

However, although the majority of Bitcoin users refer to nodes as Bitcoin miners, this is not strictly correct in the strictest meaning of the term. To be more specific, each node is participating in a competition to earn Bitcoins by solving mathematical challenges. Bitcoin was the impetus for the development of Blockchain in its current form. However, it is currently considered to be one of the many potential applications for the technology.

About 600–700 cryptocurrencies have been produced, and each one has its own set of exchangeable tokens that represent its worth. Additionally, a number of additional potential versions of the original blockchain idea are now under development or are already in use.

The Network Is Not Centralized

Decentralized systems, such as the blockchain network, are prevalent nowadays. What happens on it is a collaborative effort between everyone on it. This might have a number of significant consequences. Some elements of traditional commerce may be phased out in the process of developing a new system of validating transactions. Using the Blockchain, for example, stock market trading may become simultaneous, and other types of data recording, such as property registration, could become entirely open to the general public. There have been several decades of decentralization in place.

In order to administer the database, which contains information about Bitcoin transactions, a global network of computers use blockchain technology. The system as a whole, rather than a single administrative agency, manages Bitcoin as a result. The network may function on a peer-to-peer (P2P) basis as a result of its decentralized nature. THE FOURTH CHAPTER:

In addition to Bitcoin, the blockchain has many other uses.

As a distributed, peer-to-peer network, the Blockchain is controlled, which means that it is constantly kept and updated across a large number of computers all over the globe. Using the program, anybody may transform their computer into a "node" in this massive network, so contributing to the continued maintenance of this ongoing record of transactional information. Because of this distributed nature, many distinct versions of the Blockchain exist all over the world, making it almost difficult for anybody to change transaction information after it has been recorded in the Blockchain.

By Design, we mean that we have taken precautions to keep our information safe.

It is helpful to think about Fort Knox as a way of better visualizing the Blockchain. It is well known that Fort Knox serves as the United States' gold bullion vault. Located deep beneath Fort Knox sits a boatload of gold. If gold has to be transported, armored vehicles and personnel armed with machine guns might be used to maintain watch while the gold is being transported, if necessary. It would be incredibly difficult for a criminal to break into Fort Knox and take the gold, not just because of the heavily protected structure, but also because gold is a heavy physical material that would be impossible to transport.

When it comes to asset protection, banks (and many other organizations) have typically followed a similar strategy, keeping everything in centralized places and relying on many layers of security measures to keep their assets safe and secure. In today's world, the great majority of financial information is stored digitally in the form of data, rather than paper documents. We put our faith in banks to have the cash on hand to back up the numbers in our bank accounts, yet for the vast majority of individuals, those figures are only records of worth rather than actual cash on hand in a vault.

The majority of our financial assets do not reside in physical vaults, but rather as financial data that is saved on a bank's server, which is known as the "digital vault." Banks attempt to transform these servers into digital replicas of Fort Knox in order to protect their customer data. The fact is that in the present world of digital transactions, this centralized paradigm does not transfer well at all. Unlike breaking into Fort Knox and stealing gold, which would necessitate the use of dynamite, special equipment, escape vehicles, and Ocean's 11-style finesse, hackers are able to break into bank servers and steal financial information on a fairly regular basis by employing only computers and software. All of these concerns, including credit card fraud and identity theft, as well as data breaches, are real and present in the world of finance.

Despite the fact that banks continue to put additional levels of protection around their "digital vaults," hackers continue to breach such vaults. Fort Knox is wonderful for holding actual amounts of gold, but when we attempt to apply this approach to data in the digital domain, it starts to crumble under our feet. Let's take a step back and examine the situation. After all, we could begin to ask whether there is a better model for storing digital information and processing digital transactions that we might use instead of trying to lock down a single central server indefinitely. This is where the Blockchain technology comes into play..

Someone such as a hacker would have to change the information not only on one block but on the entire Blockchain at the same time, across the vast majority of the computers that store the information all over the world, rather than breaking into a single central server and stealing or manipulating data to change the Blockchain.

On a technical level, this would need a vast amount of computational power, which would be very difficult to achieve under the existing circumstances of the world. Blockchain systems are safe by design since there is no centralized data storage. If someone does attempt to submit a fictitious transaction, the consequences are serious. By transferring oneself Bitcoins that do not exist, the several computers that maintain the Blockchain will notice that the math does not add up and the transaction will be rejected. Unless the math is correct, the transaction will be declared illegitimate and denied, and will not be recorded in the Blockchain's record as a result.

Blockchain Technology Is Not Just for Bitcoin Any Longer

Because of its association with Bitcoin and other cryptocurrencies, blockchain technology is often thought of as being restricted to them. Nonetheless, it has a considerably greater potential for a wide range of applications, including smart contracts, crowdfunding, governance, intellectual property, healthcare, file storage, the Internet of Things, and a plethora of others, among others. In many sectors, distributed ledgers are just now being investigated for their potential as a resource and transaction management tool. For this reason, blockchain technology alone is worth investigating further for anyone interested in investing potential in developing markets. THIRD PARTY APPLICATION

Cryptocurrencies to Consider: The Most Promising as Well as the Most Established

Involvement in the Bitcoin Economy

In the previous 10 years, the value of Bitcoin has soared by orders of magnitude. At the beginning of 2011, you could acquire Bitcoin for only $0.05; but, as regular investors began to hop on the Bitcoin bandwagon, the price of Bitcoin has skyrocketed tremendously. For the first time, the price of Bitcoin exceeded $1,000 in 2014, thanks to a bull run.

In December 2017, Bitcoin had surpassed $20,000, but was in the midst of a bear market that would last until the end of the decade. After another bull run in 2021, Bitcoin reached a high of $64,000, and right now, in the second half of 2021, it is bouncing between $30,000 and $45,000, according to Bloomberg.

You must take advantage of Bitcoin's volatility and forecast price swings in order to be a successful investor and trader.

Bitcoin Is a Source of Consternation

A slew of criticism and issues have surrounded Bitcoin, despite the fact that it is the most popular cryptocurrency. Many Wall Street investors believe that Bitcoin is a speculative bubble and that it will crash in the coming months.

merely serves as a convenient means of money exchange for money launderers and criminals.

However, while it is true that Bitcoin serves as a haven for criminals, there is a strong argument that many illegal activities are carried out using real money in addition to Bitcoin. What is it about Bitcoin that has people so enraged?

Bitcoin is a powerful technology that has the potential to revolutionize technological industries while also providing a means for people in marginalized or heavily inflated economies to conduct transactions without fear of being persecuted for doing so.

Ethereum is a cryptocurrency that is used to exchange value for goods and services (ETH)

With smart contracts, Ethereum extends the real-world functionality of blockchain technology and is an open-source, decentralized cryptocurrency. Ethereum is a cryptocurrency that is decentralized and open source. A high number of transactions makes it the second most popular cryptocurrency in terms of market capitalization, and it can be considered the most active cryptocurrency as a result of its high market capitalization.

Founded by Vitalik Buterin, a former Google employee who also ran a popular Bitcoin magazine, Ethereum is a decentralized cryptocurrency platform. A popular Initial Coin

Offering (ICO) that achieved success in the cryptocurrency arena was the Ethereum project, which was launched in 2013.

What Are Smart Contracts and Why Do They Matter?

Automated triggering events that can occur in a blockchain when a particular instance occurs are known as smart contracts. High-level programming languages are typically used in the development of smart contracts, but Solidity, which was developed specifically for the Ethereum blockchain, is the most popular of these.

When developers use smart contracts to create decentralized applications, they have the potential to completely transform the world of decentralized finance. With the help of decentralized applications, Ethereum developers are experimenting with concepts such as lending cryptocurrencies and borrowing cryptocurrencies themselves.

The Native Cryptocurrency is defined as follows:

Its native cryptocurrency is called Ether (ETH), which stands for "Ethereum is a digital asset." Anyone who wishes to run a decentralized application on the platform must pay a transaction fee in Ether in order to compensate the miners who operate the platform. To reward its miners, Ethereum has relied on the Proof of Work consensus mechanism from the beginning. Despite this, the founder of Ethereum has stated in recent announcements that the Proof of Stake mechanism will be implemented over the next few years due to concerns about the environment.

Is it possible to list some of the Ethereum's applications?

Ethereum can be used by developers to create applications that can effectively monitor initial coin offerings (ICOs) and other token sales.

Ether is the most widely used Blockchain technology, with many decentralized cryptocurrency exchanges relying on it for their operations.

Ethereum, in the form of non-fungible tokens, is also the foundational Blockchain for digital art collectors (NFTs.)

Ether is also said to be extremely adaptable when it comes to decentralized applications that are centered on sports betting and gambling, among other things.

Chapter Four

Cryptocurrency investment in the form of Ethereum

Investing in Ethereum is highly recommended due to the fact that it has the most active community in the cryptocurrency industry. Ethereum has a lot of potential in the future, thanks to its second-largest market capitalization and a slew of ambitious decentralized applications in the early stages of development.

Cardano is a fictional character created by the fictional character Cardano in the year 2000. (ADA)

A new generation cryptocurrency, Cardano is focused on scalability and environmental issues, both of which have been criticised in the past for the shortcomings of previous generations. According to a tweet from Elon Musk in May 2021, Tesla cars will no longer accept Bitcoin as a payment method due to the environmental impact of the cryptocurrency.

CRYPTOCURRENCY INVESTMENT IN THE FORM OF ETHEREUM

The price of cryptocurrencies plummeted as a result of this incident.

In spite of the fact that Bitcoin has numerous advantages, it is based on the complex and energy-intensive Proof of Work consensus mechanism. According to the same rationale, China has also prohibited various cryptocurrency exchanges.

Cardinal goal is to implement a well-researched Proof of Stake algorithm that can effectively maintain multiple isolated blockchains in a decentralized environment. A large number of individuals from a variety of prestigious institutions participate in the research, which is peer reviewed.

With Cardano, the goal is to build a complex blockchain platform that is capable of efficiently running smart contracts while also providing a variety of advanced features that can be controlled by the user. As an added bonus, the Ouroboros mechanism that comes with Cardano is a fantastic addition to the active operation of complex financial applications.

What Is the Mechanism of the Ouroboros?

The Proof of Stake algorithm, also known as Ouroboros, is a more sophisticated implementation of the algorithm. During the mining process, Ouroboros selects a small number of nodes from various networks at random. They will be referred to as slot leaders.

Using the epoch concept, Cardano approaches cryptocurrency mining by segmenting the Blockchain into different slots. Mining a specific epoch in the Blockchain will typically be performed by slot leaders. Because Cardano allows for the creation of infinite epochs, it is very simple to conduct an infinite number of transactions without causing a bottleneck.

It has been stated by Cardano co-founder, Charles Hoskinson, that Cardano employs mathematical security to ensure that only a small number of nodes with high stakes are chosen as the slot leader. To combat the environmental issues that cryptocurrency is typically associated with, Cardano seeks to develop a fair and effective system.

Investing in Cardano is a good idea.

One of the most popular cryptocurrencies, Cardano has ambitious goals that could significantly alter the cryptocurrency industry as we know it. A market capitalization of nearly $2 billion places it among the top five most valuable cryptocurrencies in circulation.

Cardano, despite the fact that it is a large and ambitious project, is still in its early stages. As a result of this, many decentralized finance applications, including those powered by Ethereum, have already benefited from the services provided by its competitors. Due to the project's lack of a tangible output, it may be a source of concern for investors who are anticipating a period of volatility.

LTC is a cryptocurrency that is based on the technology known as Litecoin (LTC)

A popular peer-to-peer cryptocurrency, Litecoin was created by Charlie Lee on the basis of the open-source Bitcoin source code and has since gained widespread adoption. Because of this, Litecoin is often referred to as the "digital gold." He has stated numerous times that his intention is not to develop a cryptocurrency that will replace Bitcoin, but rather to develop a cryptocurrency that will work in conjunction with it instead.

The main reason for the development of Litecoin has been the scalability issues that have plagued Bitcoin in the past few years. When a new block in the Blockchain is validated and verified, it takes approximately 10 minutes for Bitcoin. Because of this, Litecoin reduced the block waiting time to 2.5 minutes and increased the number of coins in circulation.

The Proof of Work consensus mechanism used by Litecoin is similar to that used by Bitcoin; however, instead of employing the SHA-256 hashing algorithm, it employs a recently developed minimal hashing algorithm known as Scrypt. In Litecoin mining, the Scrypt algorithm assists miners in verifying transactions using a graphics processing unit (GPU), which is not considered a viable option for Bitcoin miners.

In addition, Litecoin is the first cryptocurrency to implement a segregated witness in its Blockchain in order to increase its efficiency. Also notable is that it is the first cryptocurrency platform to send a transaction over the Lightning Network.

Investing in Litecoin: Is It a Good Idea?

Because of its high market capitalization and large number of miners, Litecoin has consistently ranked among the top five cryptocurrencies since its launch in 2011. For a small sum of money, Litecoin is an excellent investment option. You should make certain that the community is active before making a large financial commitment, as the number of updates has decreased significantly over time.

Swelling ebb and flow (XRP)

It is claimed that Ripple is the next generation's advanced remittance and payment solution, and that it is a payment protocol. It makes use of a real-time gross settlement system, which allows transactions to be completed in seconds rather than minutes or hours. It was developed by Ripple Labs in 2012, and it has been slowly adopted by a number of large financial institutions that conduct billions of transactions every year as a result.

Ripple accepts payments in both fiat currency and cryptocurrencies at the same time. This is accomplished through the use of a distributed ledger based on blockchain technology to store all of the transaction records of Ripple account holders. Rupees (XRP) is the native cryptocurrency of

Ripple, and it is a reliable cryptocurrency that has the potential to generate significant returns.

What is the Ripple Protocol and how does it function?

In order to better understand the working model of the ripple protocol, we've provided a simple example scenario.

Banking institution A in the United States makes the decision to transfer USD 100 million to banking institution B in Japan. The majority of the time, these transactions take place in small batches, and it takes a long time to transfer all of the funds from one bank to another due to the various banking protocols used by different countries. These funds may disappear or end up in the wrong account as a result of technical malfunctions from time to time.

As a solution to these issues, the Ripple protocol first converts all fiat currency into XRP, which is the native cryptocurrency of the Ripple network, and then back again. It then transfers these native cryptocurrencies to the foreign bank's Ripple account in an almost instantaneous and low-fee process. All of the transactions will be verified by 41 independent servers that are located all over the world and are completely dependable in their verification.

Investing in Ripple is a good idea.

Ripple is a partial cryptocurrency that has expanded its services to include a number of large financial institutions, including banks. In terms of market capitalization, it ranks third in popularity after Bitcoin and Ethereum, with a market capitalization of $1 billion. Ripple, on the other hand, has a problem in that it is frequently involved in legal disputes, which makes it difficult to use. For their violations of American financial guidelines, the SEC filed lawsuits against Ripple labs in 2018 and 2020.

In contrast, Ripple Lab's founders have stated on multiple occasions that their company is transparent and that they use escrow-based services to efficiently distribute the Ripple coin supply.

Connected by a chain (LINK)

Cryptocurrencies such as Ethereum and Cardano, which use blockchain technology to create decentralized platforms, can assist developers in the development of distributed applications. In order to be efficient and to be used in the real world, these decentralized applications typically require data from the outside world.

Simple and quick to implement, using static data is a good option. Real-world applications, on the other hand, rely heavily on dynamic real-world data, which is necessary for decentralized applications to function properly. Through the use of a decentralized Oracle network, Chainlink is a cryptocurrency platform that provides real-world smart data to various blockchains. In the Chainlink platform, there is a native cryptocurrency called LINK.

In the early stages of development, Chainlink is a new third-generation cryptocurrency that is still in the early stages of development. Smart contracts can be made ten times more efficient, according to the founders, when off-chain data is used in the Chainlink platform.

In what ways does Chainlink assist you with your research?

A chainlink network makes use of a variety of nodes from reputable sources to deliver data for any purpose. In order to create decentralized gambling applications, developers can, for example, use data from football games.

All of the nodes that are currently present in Chainlink have been verified by the community and can be considered reliable sources of information.. In order to improve the reliability of the platform, Chainlink penalizes nodes that provide false information..

Is it a good idea to put money into Chainlink stock?

Despite the fact that Chainlink is a next-generation cryptocurrency, its implementation in the real world still requires a significant amount of work. The lack of actual decentralized applications means that increasing the value of LINK will take a significantly longer period of time than it would otherwise. If you want to achieve better results as an investor, you must consider Chainlink as a long-term investment.

Binance Coin is a cryptocurrency that was launched in January 2017. (BNB)

Bitcoin exchange Binance is the most well-known cryptocurrency exchange on the planet. To raise funds for their cryptocurrency exchange, the founders of Binance launched an initial coin offering (ICO) in 2016. In response to the overwhelming interest, Binance coin was made available as an ERC token on the Ethereum blockchain for a short period of time. Ticker symbols, similar to those used by stock exchanges, are assigned to tokens to identify them. The symbol for Ethereum is ETH, while the symbol for Binance Coin is BNB, and ERC is an abbreviation for Ethereum request for comment (also known as ERC-20).

Over the course of several years, Binance developed its own Blockchain and issued its own native tokens, known as "BNB," to support the ecosystem. In order to develop and improve the Binance ecosystem, a portion of the native tokens is used by Binance. In addition to allowing investors and traders to exchange cryptocurrencies with lower transaction fees, the rise in BNB prices has assisted Binance in this endeavor.

Investing in Binance: Is It a Good Idea?

Due to the rapid growth of cryptocurrency exchanges in recent years, the Binance coin is a sound investment option. Beyond its primary application, the Binance blockchain can be used to purchase virtual gifts and make charitable contributions.

THREE-THIRD CHAPTER

Stablecoin

An additional consideration is whether I have any motivation to pay for a cup of coffee with bitcoins if I am aware that it is an asset with a long-term appreciation potential.

Essentially, bitcoin is a digital currency and a store of value. Would you be willing to pay for a cup of coffee with a piece of gold? This is one of the motivations behind the creation of stable coins. This cryptocurrency, like all others, is a digital currency with a constant value, just as the name suggests. It is similar to other cryptocurrencies in that it has a fixed value. In other words, it doesn't lose value or gain in value; it stays the same value and price.

It is true that in order to trade on exchanges, you must first exchange your fiat currency (such as the dollar, the pound, or the euro) for a stable coin such as the bitcoin. As a result, you can purchase cryptocurrencies using this stable coin.

According to some definitions, a stable coin is a currency that allows users to transact on cryptocurrency exchanges.

A blockchain-based digital currency is not issued by any government agency; rather, it is created digitally in a blockchain by the company that issues it.

Will it be safe? is the question.

It is not possible for a coin's value to appear out of nowhere as if by magic; otherwise, each of us could wake up one morning and sell the coin we had dreamed of creating the night before. Was it worth anything, and more importantly, who would be willing to purchase it?

These coins are linked to a valuable asset or another currency in order to maintain their value over time.

The issuer of a stable coin should deposit a sum of money equal to the value of the coins it puts into circulation, in a one-to-one ratio, in order to ensure the coin's value remains stable.

Example: 1,000,000 stable coins = 1,000,000 dollars pledged as collateral.

Coins that are stable in value

There are many different stable currencies, each with its unique set of characteristics: some are centralized, some are decentralized, some are regulated, others are not, some are secure, and some are not safe at all (see chart).

Look at the most capitalized, and hence the most significant words together.

Then we'll analyze them individually, taking into consideration their utility and hazards.

Tether in US Dollars

As the oldest and most widely utilized of the bunch, it is also the one that gets the most criticism.

It was only in 2015 that Tether came into being; it presently has a market valuation of over $ 37 billion and is expanding at a rapid pace.

In terms of underlying collateral, it is centralized and tied to the US dollar. A 1:1 ratio should be maintained, which means that for every USDT issued, a US dollar should be deposited in its place.

It has not always been the case, however, as history has shown us. A lack of transparency from the business that provides Tether has made it impossible to ascertain how much dollars were kept in guaranteed deposits on its accounts with any confidence. Fractional reserves are permissible by the corporation, just as they are by financial institutions. That is, a liquid portion of the funds stays in the escrow account, while the remaining portion, which is the bigger portion, is allocated to loans and other investments.

The fact that a quarter of the capitalization of Tether USDT had been put in escrow accounts was known about the cryptocurrency until recently.

A debate is now happening with the federal authorities in the United States in order to certify its regulation, and it seems that they are close to reaching an agreement that is fair to all parties..

Despite all of this, USDT remains the most widely utilized and most highly capitalized stable currency on the majority of trading platforms.

One reason for its popularity is the fact that it allows users to purchase and trade almost all of the cryptocurrencies currently in circulation. At the same time, the trading opportunities for other stable currencies are significantly reduced.

TRUEUSD is a currency that stands for TrueUSD.

Founded in 2018, it has a market value of around $280,000,000 and is tied to the United States dollar. For the first time, it is controlled and the financial status of whomever is issuing it may be seen in plain sight. This stable currency, albeit newer than Tether, has great potential due of its blockchain technology.

Has everything going for him.

The standard for PAX is PAXos (Paxos).

Apart from being centralized, it also benefits from the oversight and assistance provided by the financial services department of the New York Stock Exchange, which was established in 2018. The company was founded in 2018 and has a market valuation of around $800,000,000.

Even while it has earned its trust and reputation on the one hand, it is possible that it will not take off because of this same reason in the relatively open world of cryptocurrencies.

Maker Dao is a DAI maker.

Birthday is celebrated on the first day of the month of December. 2017 is a decentralized cryptocurrency with a market valuation of around $91,000,000 that was created specifically to go against the grain, to be detached from established currencies, and to be exempt from the jurisdiction of financial regulatory bodies.

Its smart contract ensures that DAI Maker Dao continues to exist and grow on the Ethereum network while being stable.

Decentralization offers certain advantages; on the other hand, the fact that it is governed by software makes it more volatile than the others and perhaps more vulnerable to cyber-attacks than the others as a result.

More stable currencies are available, each with its own set of features and advantages over the others. However, it is not my responsibility to compile a comprehensive list and explanation of all stable coins in existence; you can easily get this information on the coin market cap website, which covers all cryptocurrencies, including stable coins, in one convenient location. It provides information about the company's major characteristics, the current price, and the total value of the stock market.

It is my hope that this lecture will help people understand what stable currencies are, why they are created, what they are used for, and why they are of significance to us.

If you want to trade on the stock market, I cannot advise you which one to utilize. My personal preference is for the first two, TUSD and USDT, which are the ones I most often use. One for the assurances it provides, and the other, despite the fact that it has received a lot of attention, for the many kinds of trading options it provides and the fact that it is accepted on the majority of exchanges.

Of course, everyone has his or her unique taste in music.

Chapter Five

The Finance Industry Is Decentralized

At the moment, DeFi is based on Ethereum, an open-source blockchain network that makes use of intelligent contracts. Essentially, a smart contract is a piece of code that runs on the Ethereum platform and is responsible for executing the code when transactions are made or received, as well as for storing all of the tokens in a public ledger that has been generated on the network. In this case, there is no need for a "middle man" since all functions are totally automated and all transactions are documented. This gives you the ability to maintain complete control over your financial activities, savings, and even investments, ensuring that everything is really yours. We all have the capacity to become our own bank, thanks to DeFi's assistance. We are in the midst of a new and developing area that will fundamentally alter how the world operates in the future. You must, however, be curious as to how DeFi works in practice. Following that, we'll go through the complete procedure of DeFi, so that you may have a better understanding of how it works in practice.

Decentralized Finance: What is it and how does it work?

While conventional financial services rely on human interaction inside the banking facility, DeFi makes use of technology to enhance the customer experience and increase efficiency. In Decentralized Finance, everything is totally automated via the use of smart contract code, as I previously said in the previous part. The two most critical aspects that must be addressed for DeFi to perform properly must be understood before beginning the DeFi process. These are as follows:

Infrastructure with a decentralized design.

Without a decentralized infrastructure, which serves as the foundation for the whole process, DeFi would not function properly. As previously said, DeFi might be developed on the Ethereum platform, which is well-known for its ability to support the development of decentralized applications (dapps). This is why you need the Ethereum platform.

Using the smart contract functionality, you may, for example, establish certain rules that outline how financial services will be offered in the future. The rules may be deployed on the Ethereum platform after they have been established. To be on the safe side, keep in mind that once a smart contract is launched on the Ethereum network, it cannot be modified since the rules of the network have already been defined.

Blockchain technology is most often used by users to create decentralized applications, or DApps, for their own financial services. Users may autonomously define their own rules for managing their financial services by using the smart contract capability. Decentralized Finance has grown increasingly accessible in recent years as a result of the decentralized infrastructure that is available on the Ethereum platform.

DeFi Currency is an abbreviation for DeFi Financial Institutions.

Without a currency system, the financial system is just another empty bone in the body of humanity. The absence of a currency with monetary worth in this world makes it impossible for anybody to do business. To bring DeFi to life, you'll also need a currency that will be used to power the financial services. There is a need for a stable currency in the case of DeFi; that is, a currency whose value does not vary significantly.

Though decentralized, cryptocurrencies are very volatile in their natural environment. Example: The Ethereum platform, which is also known as the Ethereum or ETH token, has its own cryptocurrency. ETH tokens are only problematic in that they are very volatile in nature, with price fluctuations of hundreds of percent or more. Even if Bitcoin may out to be the most advantageous alternative, the crypto token cannot be readily implemented on the Ethereum platform.

As a result, with two of our most promising options having already been ruled out, we are left with just one remaining option: stablecoins. Many individuals have recommended stablecoins since their value is fixed to the US dollar, which implies that there is less room for the price to fluctuate in an uncontrollable manner.

In order to provide an example, we may look at DAI, the world's first decentralized stablecoin, whose value is fixed to the US dollar. A DAI is equal to a dollar in terms of money, in basic words An further factor contributing to DAI's status as a stable currency is the fact that its monetary value is backed by cryptocurrency collateral rather than being directly tied to the US Dollar. So, DAI would be the ideal cryptocurrency to be utilized as DeFi money on a decentralized infrastructure, in other words.

As soon as the two most important parameters that influence the DeFi protocol have been defined and met, we can go on to the next phase, which is to understand the process, or how the DeFi truly works.

When and How Does the DeFi Process Take Place?

You should be able to get a general sense of what DeFi is based on the way it was stated in the first section, which is a peer-to-peer network that is not hindered by any government regulations. In our modern society, though, how does DeFi function? It has occurred many times: a notion seems to be effective and valuable in a textbook, but in practice, it isn't really engaging or makes any sense at all. DeFi, on the other hand, has been in use on the Ethereum platform for quite some time, and it is well-liked by the community. Some of the most important aspects to consider while learning about decentralized finance are as follows:

Intermediaries are no longer needed. By removing all middlemen from the financial system, DeFi is able to achieve total deregulation. In the eyes of many, intermediaries (often regulatory bodies that keep tabs on your every action) serve as a type of protection. A centrally planned financial system, in which banks or financial institutions backed by the authority of the Central Bank serve as middlemen. All of your transactions are safe and secure because of the financial institution's efforts; as a consequence, your money passes through them before it reaches the other party. Consequently, these intermediaries have more influence over you at the end of the day since they retain your money, and the financial system would be crippled if they were not present. By eliminating these middlemen or third parties from the financial system, Decentralized Finance can totally eradicate them from the system.

Smart Contracts are used in this case: As soon as you eliminate the middlemen from the system, you will need someone to document your transaction and maintain a record of your financial assets and liabilities. The DeFi system makes use of the smart contract functionality on the Ethereum platform, which serves as an account for the system's transactions. A smart contract will then be created to keep all of your money and spend them for the transaction in accordance with the set of instructions included inside the smart contract. In order to make every transaction as seamless and practicable as possible, DeFi uses smart contracts and cryptocurrencies in conjunction with one another. This eliminates the need for a third party or middleman.

Returns control to the user by allowing: The difficulty with a centralized system is that control is concentrated in just one hand, and that hand is that of the regulatory authority. Their position of power allows them to abuse it and, at times, ignore systemic shortcomings. DeFi has decentralized this control by developing a peer-to-peer network that facilitates the exchange of information between two individuals or groups. Meaning that you have complete control over your money and transactions, with no interference from an authority figure. With the help of DeFi, decentralized financial systems have become a reality, something that would have been impossible just a few decades before.

All-inclusive accessibility: Individuals all over the world, in certain geographic locations, are unable to access any financial services, which places a restriction on their ability to create a bank account. The absence of a bank account in the conventional financial world precludes the completion of any transaction since a bank account confirms your identification and acts as verification for all of your financial dealings. But in the realm of DeFi, one does not always have to deal with the same amount of limitations. Even individuals who do not currently have access to banks or financial institutions will be able to participate in the new financial system via the decentralized finance system, which is currently being developed by the United Nations. Last but not least, they will be given access to worldwide ways of value exchange. The eighth chapter is titled

Choosing the Proprietary Platforms

Once you have made the decision to trade in cryptocurrencies, you will need a platform that will allow you to purchase and sell cryptocurrencies easily and conveniently.

Making a list of the criteria that will guide your selection of trading platforms will help you avoid the pitfalls that many beginners experience, such as signing up for a trading platform where your preferred cryptocurrencies are not tradeable or not purchaseable with fiat currency, which is a common occurrence for beginners. This will also assist you in avoiding signing up for a platform that is not safe and is prone to getting hacked in the future as well.

The following are some characteristics to consider while determining which bitcoin trading platform is the best fit:

What is the level of security provided by the server and website?

If the cash flow is quick, then the company has good liquidity.

How much is being charged in fees and spreads for each transaction?

Transparency: How transparent is the exchange in terms of pricing, volumes, and the coins that are traded?

How many different currency pairings are there to choose from? Whether or if the platform trades the currency pairings that I choose is up to you. If so, what is the relationship between the two currencies (e.g. cryptocurrency and cryptocurrency, fiat and cryptocurrency, cryptocurrency and fiat, and so on)?

What payment methods are available for both purchasing and getting sales proceeds? What payment methods are available for both buying and receiving sales proceeds?

Does customer service provide what it promises? Customer satisfaction levels are high. When it comes to client service, how quickly and effectively does it operate? The most often encountered client grievances are as follows:

What is the current rating of the trading platform in terms of reputation?

Does the platform provide a user-friendly environment for newcomers? What resources does it have to assist new traders in learning how to trade on its platform? Are dummy accounts available so that new traders may practice until they are confident enough to trade on the platform?

With the right parameters in mind, you may now choose the most suitable platform. Some of the greatest platforms to consider are listed below:

Binance

If you look at the total trading volume, Binance is one of the most significant cryptocurrency exchanges. An individual by the name of Changpen Zhao founded the cryptocurrency exchange Binance, which launched in China in 2017. With time, it has earned a reputation as one of the most dependable cryptocurrency exchanges in the world. Because of the difficulties that Binance has encountered in China, the exchange is now based in the European territory of Malta. The company also created a platform called Binance US, which is devoted only to the United States and is compatible with the regulatory framework in place in the United States, in September 2019.

The cryptocurrency exchange, Binance, is also one of the few platforms that does not have fictitious trade volume or even wash trading activity. This indicates that the organization is very transparent and open. In business, the greater the amount of openness available, the better.

Binance has also placed a strong emphasis on keeping up with the newest software and technology, ensuring that it remains competitive in an industry that is always evolving. It has managed to position itself as one of the most widely used gateways in the cryptocurrency market.

Coinbase

Cryptocurrency trading platform Coinbase is the most widely used in the industry. According to the vast majority of bitcoin users, it is the most reliable cryptocurrency trading site. The platform facilitates the trading of the majority of the top cryptocurrencies.

In the period from October to November 2017, Coinbase saw an approximately sevenfold increase in traffic. Around 20 million bitcoin wallets and 75,000 businesses that utilize the platform as a payment processor were on its books by the middle of 2017. The company also boasted 15,000 app developers who have built APIs on its platform.

Bittrex

When it comes to new currency and user security, Bittrex is well-known for its thorough screening procedure. In addition, it has a high-security module in place. A diverse range of currencies is also supported. Trading in over 190 digital currencies is now supported. A high degree of stability is combined with a high level of responsiveness in transactional processing. This wallet is one of the most secure on the market because of its high degree of protection.

This has been predicted by several bitcoin experts as the cryptocurrency exchange that would eventually overtake Coinbase. With dealers from over 180 nations participating, it is the most globally integrated exchange platform. Due to a partnership with online payment and verification provider Jumio, this has been made feasible for the company. Coinbase, on the other hand, is struggling to service customers in North America, Europe, Australia and Singapore due to a lack of infrastructure. While it competes in the United States, Europe, and Japan, its junior rival Kraken exclusively serves those three regions.

When it comes to traffic, Bittrex has already exceeded Coinbase, with more than 160 million visits each month, as opposed to Coinbase, which gets around 125 million visitors per month. A total of 45 million people visit Kraken each year.

Almost as much as Coinbase and Kraken combined, it gets the biggest level of mobile traffic (35 percent).

Kraken

With a high-security foundation, Kraken can be trusted. This platform is used by intermediate and professional traders because of its quick financing and strong liquidity. It also offers leveraged trading, minimal fees, and advanced orders such as stop-loss orders. Both fiat cash and cryptocurrency transactions are accepted on the site, and they may be completed by a wire transfer to the bank in question. Neither cash nor debit/credit cards, however, are accepted on the site.

Cex

A holding company for one of the world's biggest Bitcoin mining businesses, GHash, Cex was established in the United Kingdom. With around 42 percent of Bitcoin hashing power, GHash is the dominant force in the cryptocurrency industry. In the United Kingdom, Cex is based. Traders may make deposits in US Dollars, Russian Rubles, and Euros via credit cards, SEPA transfers, and wire transfer services. User transactions from all across the world, whether they are trading in Bitcoins or GHash mining shares, are accepted by this exchange. When Bitcoin Cash (BCH), a fork of the original Bitcoin, was introduced, Cex was one of the first sites to accept it.

Coinmama

When it comes to trading, Coinmama is a user-friendly platform that does not need the user to hold any cryptocurrency. Starting with fiat cash, new cryptocurrency buyers may get their feet wet. It is possible to access this platform from almost any country in the globe.

Trading Platforms that are not as well-known

Bitstamp.net LocalBitcoins Gemini is a cryptocurrency exchange based in Gemini, Arizona. Cryptocurrency exchanges Bitfinex Bisq Bitstamp CEX.IO eToro Poloniex Bitfinex Bisq Bitstamp CEX.IO Poloniex Bitfinex Bisq Bitstamp BTC-e, BitMEX-e, and GDAX-e are examples of cryptocurrency exchanges. Etherdelta.com Paxful.com\sCoinATMradar.com

how to become a member of an investment and trading platform

Register with the trading platform of your choice. 2Factor authentication should be enabled when necessary.

Continue to compare other cryptocurrencies to Bitcoin on a regular basis. Concentrate on maximizing your profit margins.

Keep an ear out for industry influencers and opinion shapers to see what they are saying. Consider the fact that you will be taxed. THIRD PARTY:

A Guide to Wallets and How to Pick One

There are several traits that are shared by all digital wallets: There will be a public key, a private key, and an interface that will let you to examine your transaction history, security choices, and available money for each wallet. It is the liquidity and security that will be the most noticeable variations between the two. These two characteristics are often in conflict with one another. For example, the more secure your cryptocurrency is, the less liquidity it has, and the converse.

It is a little deceptive to refer to Bitcoin as a wallet since it is not physically housed in a wallet, as it would be with actual money. In order to engage with the block change, you just need to use the wallet. Physical coins are never traded or exchanged in any way.

When it comes to storing your Bitcoin, you have a handful of choices. You could store your coins on an exchange, or you could store your coins on your computer's hard drive, or you might store them in a cold wallet. This will depend on your attitude to security, how important liquidity is to you, and your overall investing plan, among other considerations. The advantages and disadvantages of each of these alternatives will be discussed in detail below.

Keeping it on the market is Option 1.

Its advantage is that it provides the most liquid alternative accessible to you, which is a big plus in this case. They are user-friendly, and you can withdraw your funds at any moment. Cryptocurrency exchanges are generally secure, and you may withdraw funds at any time. The fact that exchanges may be hacked, making them less secure than the other solutions, should not be overlooked.

It will be necessary to utilize a cryptocurrency exchange, such as Gemini or Coinbase, in order to convert your dollars into Bitcoin when making your first Bitcoin purchase. After you make a purchase on the exchange of your choice, it will automatically establish a wallet for you without your involvement.

Every trade, on the other hand, is not created equal, and some are more reliable than others. Exchanges are seldom compromised, but they are clearly a target for resourceful cybercriminals.

While this is the greatest choice for those who are interested in trading coins on a daily basis, it is important to note that doing so is not recommended due to the high risk of losing money.

Only two-factor authentication is required in order to keep your money in a cryptocurrency exchange's vault! You don't have to worry about anything else.

Wallet made of metal (option 2)

Choosing this option will provide you with the greatest level of security and peace of mind. Although they are typically more costly, physical wallets are far less liquid than digital wallets and need significantly more time to trade currencies.

Security experts consider a hardware wallet to be the gold standard. You must acquire anything that will allow you to directly invest your coins using a device that only you will have access to in order to do this. When compared to a software wallet, it offers a plethora of benefits.

A hardware wallet's private keys are typically kept in a secure location and are not accessible outside of the hardware wallet itself. As an added security measure, these hardware wallets are resistant to the kinds of viruses that may steal from a software wallet.

Unlike paper wallets, which must be imported into software, hardware wallets may be utilized securely and interactively, which is not possible with paper wallets.

Up to this moment, there have been no confirmed cases of bitcoin being taken from hardware wallets of any kind. Purchasing an old wallet that has still been compromised by a hacker is the only way for this to occur since the thief will be able to take any money you deposit into it.

Once you've made a decision, you may either import an existing wallet or create a new one. PIN codes should be chosen carefully, so that they are easy to recall. Install the applications on your computer and begin using the gadget to gain access to your wallet's information. Many Chrome extensions make it quite simple to do this task.

In order to receive and transmit bitcoin, you must choose the most secure storage option available on this device.

Soft Wallets are the third option to consider.

Although they are simple to use, soft wallets offer a high level of protection. These cryptocurrencies, however, are susceptible to virus, keylogger, and malware infection, and they may not always be the best choice if you are looking to invest in a cryptocurrency that is not Bitcoin. Quality of software varies from one brand to another as well as within a brand.

Soft wallets differ from any other hardware wallets in that they do not rely on any physical tokens, instead relying solely on software to perform their function. In terms of soft wallets, there are three different types to choose from: online, desktop, and mobile applications.

Using custom software designed specifically for Bitcoin, you can access your desktop wallet. The high popularity of Bitcoin has resulted in a plethora of custom soft wallets being developed for it. Although even the most secure soft wallet is less secure than a hardware wallet, hackers can gain access to your desktop wallet through the use of keyloggers or malicious software.

Installing desktop wallet software from a reputable Bitcoin source is the first step in configuring your desktop wallet.

This software should be installed on your computer and then opened up. Even though every desktop wallet is a little different, you will have a variety of options for creating a wallet and then getting access to it at the very least. Following your login, you will be able to view your transaction history as well as the funds that are currently available.

It is then necessary for you to decrypt your wallet. This is accomplished by copying and pasting the private key you have into the wallet application.

Always make an effort to keep your antivirus software up to date so that you can be protected against any attacks on your software wallets and other sensitive information..

Chapter Six

Payment Methods Through the Internet

In comparison to exchanges, online wallets are much more secure and simple to use, with a variety of options for you to unlock your wallet. But hackers frequently target them with phishing scams, and your private key file will need to be copied and pasted in order to protect yourself. Anywhere you have access to a computer and the internet, you can decrypt your online wallet. All you need is a computer and the internet to do so.

Online wallets allow you to navigate to a website where you can interact with the Blockchain running on that website by decrypting your private key, which can be accomplished in a variety of ways depending on the wallet.

The following will serve as an example, just for the sake of clarity: My Ether Wallet

When you first visit MEW, you will be presented with a clickthrough tutorial on how to use the website. This clickthrough will also highlight its limitations and purpose, as well as provide you with the option of following along with a walkthrough to set up your wallet, despite the fact that this process is extremely straightforward.

Even so, the risk associated with using an online wallet is the same as the risk associated with using a desktop wallet, as previously stated. The use of malware by hackers to steal your private keys, copy and paste them into a different location, is a common practice.

When you create an online wallet, you will need to copy and paste the private key, which means you will need to store it in a Word document. This opens the door to new ways for hackers to try and attack you and steal your vital data.

Use of an online wallet requires the following steps to be completed. Despite the fact that other online wallets operate in the same way, I will continue to use MEW as an illustration.

Use Google to look up the name and then click on the homepage website that comes up. After going through each notice that MEW provides that explains how the website works, you can start creating your wallet and setting a password for yourself.

It is necessary to download the Keystore File after that. This will allow you to decrypt your wallet in the same way that a private key would, so if anyone gains access to it or if you misplace it, you will be putting your Bitcoin at risk of being compromised. Please save this file to a USB flash drive, preferably in a waterproof bag or container, and keep it hidden and safe at all times.

After that, select "I understand, continue," and you'll be shown your private key for confirmation. Print out this key and keep it in your paper wallet for safekeeping. Protect and store this document on your USB stick for future reference.

MEW will then provide you with a number of options for accessing your wallet account. The private key can either be uploaded as a Keystore file or copied and pasted into the field provided. In my opinion, using the Keystore file is far more secure than using the copy and paste command because malware cannot attack the file.

wallet on your phone

However, if your mobile device is ever lost or stolen, you may find yourself in serious trouble. Mobile wallets are accessible, secure, and extremely convenient digital wallets. Using an application on your mobile phone, a mobile wallet is created and operated. They allow you to receive and send cryptocurrency directly from your phone.... Numerous apps in this category integrate with hardware wallets, which are becoming increasingly popular.

A mobile wallet stores the private keys on the app and allows users to make purchases using their mobile devices (such as their smartphones). I believe this is the direction in which cryptocurrency wallets are headed, and I believe that mobile wallets will become widely used in the near future. Simply downloading and installing the mobile wallet application on your phone, then going through the necessary setup steps, is all it takes to start using a mobile wallet. Incorporate two-factor authentication if necessary.

4. Cold Wallet (also known as Option 4).

Despite the fact that cold wallets are extremely secure against malware and hackers, they may not be the most convenient option available to you at this time. In the event that the paper on which they are stored is lost or destroyed, they will require a backup solution.

It is possible to create a cold wallet when your private key is kept secure and off-line in a secure environment such as a paper wallet. This is the process by which you print out your private key on a piece of paper and store it offline, away from any internet connection.

Due to the fact that the only way to obtain your information would be to physically obtain that piece of paper and then decrypt your wallet in order to obtain your funds, this option is extremely secure. Anyone who discovers your private key will be unable to steal your funds if you keep your paper wallet hidden securely and safely.

If your paper wallet is stolen, whether by accident or on purpose, you will not be able to recover your money or documents. Therefore, it is critical to have two copies of your paper wallet stored in two different locations, both of which are high-security environments. A personal safe at home is used by some, and a lockbox is rented for the second version, which is kept at a secure location.

How to Make Use of a Cold Wallet (with Pictures)

In the event that you choose to print a paper copy of your public address and private key, make sure to store them in a waterproof container that is kept safely out of the way.

Ensure that you do not become complacent with your security measures now that you have chosen your digital wallet! Because you have taken on the role of your bank, it is your responsibility to ensure that everything is safe and secure at all times, including online. The Tenth Chapter (Chapter Ten)

Cryptocurrency Mining is a type of mining that takes place on a computer or in a network of computers.

The greater the processing power of the machine you use, which is measured in hashes per second, the more likely it is that you will complete proof of work models, and the greater the amount of money you stand to make as a result of your success. This type of cryptographic algorithm hashcash, which is based on the hash function at its core, is the most widely used proof of work model today. In order to prevent blocks from being created faster than the blockchain can handle, hashcash proofs can be set to a specific difficulty level. This difficulty level needs to be determined by the number of transactions that can be successfully processed per second. For example, a new Bitcoin block is only created every 10 minutes, according to the cryptocurrency. It is virtually impossible to predict when a specific machine will generate a new block because the probability of successful generation is extremely low.

That block must have a hash value that is greater than the hash value of the block before it in order for it to be considered valid. This means that each block contains the work that was done to create it by nature, and that each block contains the work that was done to create it. When this happens, each block includes a hash of the preceding block, which allows the chain to determine where each individual block belongs in the chain. The result is that changing a single block requires redoing all of the work that has been done on each and every subsequent block in the chain of commands.

Start Participating in the Mining Industry.

The specifics of the system you end up with will vary depending on the time period you live in, but one thing that will never change is the fact that you will require dedicated hardware in order to mine cryptocurrency efficiently. However, while it is technically still possible to mine using a computer's video card or a laptop's CPU, the speed with which modern mining machines can complete proof of work transactions means that you would be unlikely to complete even a single verification in a year.

Known for producing the highest-quality products, ASIC is capable of achieving speeds that are roughly a hundred times faster than those achieved by the average computer. For the most part, mining without the use of specialized software will result in you paying more for electricity than you will ultimately earn from the endeavor. The average mining machine costs between $500 and $4,000 as of fall 2017, with more expensive machines yielding a higher return on investment.

Once you have your mining machine in hand, the next step is to download the appropriate mining software to use with it. Several different versions of this software are currently available for purchase.... The fact that not all cryptocurrencies are compatible with each other means that you should research the specifics of your desired cryptocurrency before making a decision. Some of the most widely used versions of the software are CGminer and BFGminer, while others, such as EasyMiner, are suitable for those who are not confident in running software from the command line.

Once you have the necessary software in place, the next step is to find a mining pool to join in order to maximize your mining power and profit potential. A mining pool is a group of miners who have banded together to ensure that they can mine as many blocks as possible in a given time period. It is technically possible to mine without participating in a mining pool, but because of the complexity of the average proof-of-work model, doing so is by far the most profitable way to make money from the process. When you join a mining pool, you will be eligible to receive a share of the profits from each block that your machine contributes to verify, which is determined by one of several different payment models.

The core client for the blockchain that you will be interacting with must be downloaded if you decide to go it alone, as it is required to ensure that your version of the blockchain is in sync with the blockchain prime. If you are working with a cryptocurrency, you can usually find this information on the main website for that cryptocurrency. To avoid this situation, you should consider joining a pool instead. All you need to do is make sure to follow all of the rules and regulations that the pool sets forth, as well as to do your best to adhere to any rules and regulations that the pool sets forth.

The validation space is currently flooded with a plethora of different types of mining pools, making it difficult to find the one that is best suited to your needs. First and foremost, you should research the pools you are considering on the relevant subreddit, in order to keep the process as simple as possible. This will ensure that you have the opportunity to read about each pool before committing to anything and will prevent you from signing up for a lemon. However, while joining a popular pool will almost always result in you being eligible for more blocks, your average payout per block is going to be lower compared to joining a smaller pool. According to conventional wisdom, mining in larger numbers of smaller pools to ensure that sufficient proofs are constantly generated is better for a blockchain's health than mining in smaller pools alone.

When researching different pools, you will want to pay close attention to any information provided about how payment is generated, as this is a much more complicated process than it may appear at first glance. There are a plethora of different payment methods available, and it's a good idea to become familiar with the most commonly used types in order to avoid being stuck with something you won't enjoy in the long run.

Miners are paid for their share of the work as soon as the block is verified using the pay per share (PPS) model, which pays a specific amount for each portion of the proof that was generated by their machine. Instead of waiting for the payment to be processed by the blockchain, miners are paid from the pool's total holdings, which is a significant advantage. It is preferred by miners because it ensures that the profits generated by each block are highly consistent, and it shifts all of the risk in the event that something goes wrong to the pool's management. Because there is always the possibility that a block will not payout and will instead be orphaned, the pool operator runs the risk of not being compensated for the work performed in the long run after having already paid the miners from the pool's funds. The operator must also have a significant amount of excess capital on hand in order to ensure that they can continue to operate in the face of economic downturns. Consequently, the PPS model is no longer considered to be a standard practice.

An approach based on proportions is used. The proportional mining approach distributes mining rewards to miners in proportion to the portion of the block that their machine contributed to the creation of.. Payments are then generated after payments for the block in question have been generated previously.

In contrast to the proportional method, the pay per last N share (PPLN) model generates profit margins based on N shares instead of true shares, which is similar to the proportional method. When compared to the PPS model, a N share pays out at a variable rate based on the amount of reward received from the block in question, which means that the amount each miner receives will fluctuate depending on the results of the transaction. Afterwards, once the reward for the block has been received, the payments are sent out.

GEOMETRIC TRIANGULATION When it comes to mining payments, the double geometric payment method is a type of hybrid approach that distributes risk between a mining pool operator and individual miners. When things are going well, the pool operator retains a portion of the profits and uses those funds to compensate miners when things aren't going as smoothly as anticipated. Payments made through this system are generated based on the number of shares held, and payments are made once a block has been successfully added to the chain of communication.

Pay-sharing at the maximum: This updated version of the PPS model, known as the shared maximum pay share model (SMPPS), is becoming increasingly popular due to the way it reduces risk for the pool operator. It pays out a reward per share that is calculated based on how much money the pool has made in the most recent period of time Upon the assumption that all relevant blocks have been accepted into the chain, payments are made according to a predefined schedule.

In the recent shared maximum pay per share model (RSMPSS), newer pool members are given preference over those who have been in the pool for the longest period of time. As a result, they are more likely to receive a larger number of shares than those who have been in the pool for the longest period of time. After all of the verified blocks have been successfully added to the chain, payments are made at predetermined intervals.

Capped pay per share with recent back pay model of payment (CPPSRB): The capped pay per share with recent back pay model of payment (CPPSRB) is a variation of the standard MPPS payment method that pays miners as much as possible based on the rewards generated while first and foremost ensuring that the pool remains financially solvent. Afterwards, once the reward for the block has been received, the payments are sent out.

The pooled mining model (PMM), also known as the slush pool, is a payment model in which the final shares of a given proof of work model are paid at a higher rate than the earlier shares, which are naturally easier to generate. It is a type of payment model used in the bitcoin network. Because the rewards are lower in comparison to the amount of work being completed, this payment model is particularly effective at preventing miners from abandoning a job after half way through its duration. Afterwards, once the reward for the block has been received, the payments are sent out.

Individual miners are compensated based on the resources they used in order to generate the proof of work model as a whole in the pay on target (POT) payment method, which is yet another variation on the PPS payment method. Only after all of the relevant blocks have been verified are payments made according to a predetermined schedule.

A special reward system called SCORE is used in the SCORE payment model, and shares are weighted differently depending on how quickly the block was mined in total. As a result, it pays more for later shares of any block to compensate for the additional resources that are required to complete it. Following that, payments are generated based on the scores achieved by each miner during the proof of concept process. The reward for the block is received first, and then the payments are made.

Eligius: The eligius model of payment was developed by the owner of the BFG miner in an effort to improve upon the standard PPS model of compensation. In order to create a payment model that allows miners to be paid immediately for their work, it takes advantage of both the PPS and the BPM models' strengths and weaknesses. Each miner is compensated according to an equation that takes the total reward for a given block and divides it evenly among all the shares that were used to generate the block, while also accounting for any users who have shares of stale blocks in the current proof of work. When a stale block is produced, the shares of the miners who participated in it are rolled over into the next successfully completed block. The eleventh chapter of the book of Genesis is entitled

Staking\sBeautiful, Not at all, I believe.

In the same way that banks used to pay interest to account holders in exchange for keeping their money in the account, today it is account holders who are required to pay the banks in order to keep their money in their accounts.

By selecting "staking" from the top-level menu, a page displaying the currencies that can be rented appears.

Simply enter the amount you wish to bind in this staking account and click "Confirm." Staking is extremely simple to set up. This is accomplished by deducting the staking amount from the spot account and depositing it into the staking account

Reversing the process will result in a similar result.

It is extremely simple to use, has no commissions, and is extremely convenient for those who want to generate income from the coins they do not use on a consistent basis.

The annuity percentages are good, and they vary depending on the currency and staking plan that is selected..

THIRD PARTY APPLICATION:

To Begin, Consider

In a couple of ways, cryptocurrency trading differs from traditional investing. There are two main reasons for this: first, the market is open around the clock, meaning that anything could potentially happen even while you are sleeping. Secondly, because the market does not adhere to a traditional trading pattern, it is difficult to predict what will happen to the currency in the near future with accuracy. It is still in its infancy that digital cash, which is primarily used for investment rather than for purchases at this time, is being used for investment purposes. No one can predict the path that cryptos will take, let alone which ones will be taken by which particular ones. Consequently, cryptocurrency speculation, no matter how well-intentioned, is fraught with perilous consequences. Three-fold, it is highly volatile, and it can go from extreme highs to extreme lows in a short period of time before regaining equilibrium.

There might be some adjustments to your way of thinking if you've never traded before. Maintain your focus on the facts and not on your emotions when making investment decisions. To put it another way, when you are trading, do not allow yourself to be influenced by what is happening with your cryptocurrency by acting quickly and impulsively. Please keep in mind that the value of these currencies can fluctuate between extreme highs and extreme lows in a matter of hours and that they do not necessarily cash out overnight without being considered objective. Investing based on emotion can result in you selling your investments too soon, only to discover that they have increased exponentially the following day. What might be considered disadvantages by some can be turned into advantages by others who have the right frame of mind about the situation.

Create a list of your objectives

Making a decision about your financial objectives is the first step in investing. Investing is a complicated process; do you have a specific strategy? You might want to go away for a vacation or even to attend a wedding. If you are looking for investments that are not time-sensitive, cryptocurrency may be a good option for your needs. Because cryptocurrency is highly unpredictable, it may be difficult to plan for the future with it. It is possible to trade cryptocurrency in the short and medium term, but the risk is reduced the longer you allow your investment to grow in the cryptocurrency market. Even though cryptocurrency is not your typical investment, it may be a valuable addition to your portfolio in the future. However, relying on it for your entire retirement would be extremely risky.

People who invest in cryptocurrency do so with the intention of holding onto their investments for a long time. If you're a member of the Bitcoin community, you've probably heard the term 'HODL' mentioned in online forums. Many long-term investors in the coin have adopted this as their motto, which was inspired by a typographical error in the word "hold." Take, for example, the long-term growth of Bitcoin and Ether, two of the most established cryptocurrencies, which have experienced tremendous growth since Bitcoin was only $426.84 and Ether only $7.10 at the time of their creation (Stastica, 2021.) Due to the fact that cryptocurrency investors have shown patience, now is a good time to invest in cryptocurrencies. Numerous 'HODL' adherents are extremely optimistic about the coin's future, and even in times when its value has plummeted dramatically, they refuse to sell. Because the coin's price has frequently bounced back even higher than it was before, many of them have reaped the benefits of doing so. Theoretically, you have not lost any money until you withdraw it at a loss, and for many people who have invested in cryptocurrency, this appears to be the mindset they have taken on board. The beauty of long-term investments is that they have a long period of time in which to grow, allowing a relatively small amount of money to grow significantly with little risk to you.

Choosing the type of investment you want to make

Investing in a lump sum every month, or investing in both, is your preference. The fact that you are investing in a lump sum means that you will have to identify a good entry point into the market by studying charts and statistics, but this is doable. It is possible to even out and reduce the risk associated with fluctuating cryptocurrency prices by making a defined monthly crypto deposit; however, this may result in higher fees. The option of combining both is also a viable one. It is true that the healthier and more diverse your investment portfolio is, the lower the risk you will be exposed to.

Determine how much money you can afford to invest, taking into account the various fees and taxes that will be incurred during the process. To ensure that you get the most out of your investment, make sure that the money you use can be committed to your investments for a long period of time in order to minimize the losses you may incur if you withdraw it too soon. Keep in mind that even a small sum of $200, if invested correctly and over a long period of time, can grow into a substantial sum of money. Therefore, no amount of money is too small to invest.

To give an extreme example, on January 1st, 2021, Dogecoin was worth $0.0o54 and, after a rollercoaster of highs, it finally corrected in July to a value of between $.32 and $.38, according to coinmarketcap.com. If you had invested $200 in the coin in January, your money would now be worth at least $11,851.85 before fees and taxes, assuming no fees and taxes were deducted from your earnings. The amount of money you have invested can therefore grow exponentially in some instances.

Making a few inquiries.

Other costs must be taken into consideration when determining an acceptable return on your investments. Keep in mind that your initial returns will be in gross, not net, format, and that deductions will reduce your overall profit margin. The majority of investments, for example, generate capital gains tax on their profits, and other taxes may be applicable depending on where you reside. It is possible to incur these taxes when moving currencies around, so keep this in mind before moving your cryptocurrency around without a reason. Keep in mind that there may be fees associated with the exchange or broker you choose, so do your homework first. There may also be fees associated with receiving a payout into your bank account or PayPal, so make sure to look into these in advance based on your specific requirements and requirements.

Consider what kind of return would be acceptable after taxes and fees. In order to make it worthwhile to make a small investment, the return on that investment should be high enough before you try to withdraw it. Making a healthy profit and having it nearly completely absorbed by fees, taxes, and transaction costs is a complete waste of time. There are a variety of services and types of wallets available to help you keep track of your cryptocurrency investments. You can set alerts to notify you when your cryptocurrency has reached a target price, which can be particularly useful if you are investing for a shorter period of time.

Taking a broad view of the market,

Trying to claim that the market is predictable and easy to follow would be a lie. The market is extremely volatile and driven by so many variables that a significant portion of the entire process is simply a matter of chance. But by gaining an understanding of the overall sentiment expressed in the markets, some good indicators can give you an indication of when there may be good investment opportunities ahead.

Following both the stock market and cryptocurrency news will give you an indication of how optimistic or pessimistic the market is currently. Are there any signs that the market is sagging broadly? Compare the cryptocurrency market's performance with that of the equity markets. What is the current strength of fiat currencies? All of this should be kept in mind when looking at the charts of various cryptocurrencies and deciding whether you believe the overall market is a 'bullish' or a "bearish." A 'bullish' sentiment indicates that prices are currently rising and are likely to continue to rise in the near term. A 'bearish,' or pessimistic market attitude could indicate that prices are lower or less resistant to increasing, and that the market is in a low-cyclical period. Although it sounds gloomy, the term "bearish" can indicate a good buying opportunity at a reasonable price depending on where the currency is in its cycle at the time and how long you are willing to keep your money in the market for.THIRD PARTY APPLICATION:

To Begin, Consider

In a couple of ways, cryptocurrency trading differs from traditional investing. There are two main reasons for this: first, the market is open around the clock, meaning that anything could potentially happen even while you are sleeping. Secondly, because the market does not adhere to a traditional trading pattern, it is difficult to predict what will happen to the currency in the near future with accuracy. It is still in its infancy that digital cash, which is primarily used for investment rather than for purchases at this time, is being used for investment purposes. No one can predict the path that cryptos will take, let alone which ones will be taken by which particular ones. Consequently, cryptocurrency speculation, no matter how well-intentioned, is fraught with perilous consequences. Three-fold, it is highly volatile, and it can go from extreme highs to extreme lows in a short period of time before regaining equilibrium.

There might be some adjustments to your way of thinking if you've never traded before. Maintain your focus on the facts and not on your emotions when making investment decisions. To put it another way, when you are trading, do not allow yourself to be influenced by what is happening with your cryptocurrency by acting quickly and impulsively. Please keep in mind that the value of these currencies can fluctuate between extreme highs and extreme lows in a matter of hours and that they do not necessarily cash out overnight without being considered objective. Investing based on emotion can result in you selling your investments too soon, only to discover that they have increased exponentially the following day. What might be considered disadvantages by some can be turned into advantages by others who have the right frame of mind about the situation.

Create a list of your objectives

Making a decision about your financial objectives is the first step in investing. Investing is a complicated process; do you have a specific strategy? You might want to go away for a vacation or even to attend a wedding. If you are looking for investments that are not time-sensitive, cryptocurrency may be a good option for your needs. Because cryptocurrency is highly unpredictable, it may be difficult to plan for the future with it. It is possible to trade cryptocurrency in the short and medium term, but the risk is reduced the longer you allow your investment to grow in the cryptocurrency market. Even though cryptocurrency is not your typical investment, it may be a valuable addition to your portfolio in the future. However, relying on it for your entire retirement would be extremely risky.

People who invest in cryptocurrency do so with the intention of holding onto their investments for a long time. If you're a member of the Bitcoin community, you've probably heard the term 'HODL' mentioned in online forums. Many long-term investors in the coin have adopted this as their motto, which was inspired by a typographical error in the word "hold." Take, for example, the long-term growth of Bitcoin and Ether, two of the most established cryptocurrencies, which have experienced tremendous growth since Bitcoin was only $426.84 and Ether only $7.10 at the time of their creation (Stastica, 2021.) Due to the fact that cryptocurrency investors have shown patience, now is a good time to invest in cryptocurrencies. Numerous 'HODL' adherents are extremely optimistic about the coin's future, and even in times when its value has plummeted dramatically, they refuse to sell. Because the coin's price has frequently bounced back even higher than it was before, many of them have reaped the benefits of doing so. Theoretically, you have not lost any money until you withdraw it at a loss, and for many people who have invested in cryptocurrency, this appears to be the mindset they have taken on board. The beauty of long-term investments is that they have a long period of time in which to grow, allowing a relatively small amount of money to grow significantly with little risk to you.

Choosing the type of investment you want to make

Investing in a lump sum every month, or investing in both, is your preference. The fact that you are investing in a lump sum means that you will have to identify a good entry point into the market by studying charts and statistics, but this is doable. It is possible to even out and reduce the risk associated with fluctuating cryptocurrency prices by making a defined monthly crypto deposit; however, this may result in higher fees. The option of combining both is also a viable one. It is true that the healthier and more diverse your investment portfolio is, the lower the risk you will be exposed to.

Determine how much money you can afford to invest, taking into account the various fees and taxes that will be incurred during the process. To ensure that you get the most out of your investment, make sure that the money you use can be committed to your investments for a long period of time in order to minimize the losses you may incur if you withdraw it too soon. Keep in mind that even a small sum of $200, if invested correctly and over a long period of time, can grow into a substantial sum of money. Therefore, no amount of money is too small to invest.

To give an extreme example, on January 1st, 2021, Dogecoin was worth $0.0o54 and, after a rollercoaster of highs, it finally corrected in July to a value of between $.32 and $.38, according to coinmarketcap.com. If you had invested $200 in the coin in January, your money would now be worth at least $11,851.85

before fees and taxes, assuming no fees and taxes were deducted from your earnings. The amount of money you have invested can therefore grow exponentially in some instances.

Making a few inquiries.

Other costs must be taken into consideration when determining an acceptable return on your investments. Keep in mind that your initial returns will be in gross, not net, format, and that deductions will reduce your overall profit margin. The majority of investments, for example, generate capital gains tax on their profits, and other taxes may be applicable depending on where you reside. It is possible to incur these taxes when moving currencies around, so keep this in mind before moving your cryptocurrency around without a reason. Keep in mind that there may be fees associated with the exchange or broker you choose, so do your homework first. There may also be fees associated with receiving a payout into your bank account or PayPal, so make sure to look into these in advance based on your specific requirements and requirements.

Consider what kind of return would be acceptable after taxes and fees. In order to make it worthwhile to make a small investment, the return on that investment should be high enough before you try to withdraw it. Making a healthy profit and having it nearly completely absorbed by fees, taxes, and transaction costs is a complete waste of time. There are a variety of services and types of wallets available to help you keep track of your cryptocurrency investments. You can set alerts to notify you when your cryptocurrency has reached a target price, which can be particularly useful if you are investing for a shorter period of time.

Taking a broad view of the market,

Trying to claim that the market is predictable and easy to follow would be a lie. The market is extremely volatile and driven by so many variables that a significant portion of the entire process is simply a matter of chance. But by gaining an understanding of the overall sentiment expressed in the markets, some good indicators can give you an indication of when there may be good investment opportunities ahead.

Following both the stock market and cryptocurrency news will give you an indication of how optimistic or pessimistic the market is currently. Are there any signs that the market is sagging broadly? Compare the cryptocurrency market's performance with that of the equity markets. What is the current strength of fiat currencies? All of this should be kept in mind when looking at the charts of various cryptocurrencies and deciding whether you believe the overall market is a 'bullish' or a "bearish." A 'bullish' sentiment indicates that prices are currently rising and are likely to continue to rise in the near term. A 'bearish,' or pessimistic market attitude could indicate that prices are lower or less resistant to increasing, and that the market is in a low-cyclical period. Although it sounds gloomy, the term "bearish" can indicate a good buying opportunity at a reasonable price depending on where the currency is in its cycle at the time and how long you are willing to keep your money in the market for.

CPSIA information can be obtained
at www.ICGtesting.com
Printed in the USA
LVHW020807130522
718694LV00006B/191